# Life, Love, Lies

## Fonkeng E.f

*Langaa Research & Publishing CIG*
*Mankon, Bamenda*

*Publisher:*
*Langaa* RPCIG
Langaa Research & Publishing Common Initiative Group
P.O. Box 902 Mankon
Bamenda
North West Region
Cameroon
Langaagrp@gmail.com
www.langaa-rpcig.net


Distributed in and outside N. America by African Books Collective
orders@africanbookscollective.com
www.africanbookscollective.com


*ISBN-10: 9956792586*

*ISBN-13: 9789956792580*

DISCLAIMER
All views expressed in this publication are those of the author and do not necessarily reflect the views of Langaa RPCIG.

# Dedication

*The Family Tree*

*From Past to Future*

*Every Branch*

*And Fruit therein*

# Introductory Note

*Life, Love, Lies* is a collection of reflections on perhaps the two most mundane yet fundamental aspects of human existence: love and the concept of living. In between, are matters benign and not so benign – on life – amassed, experienced and/or lived, for well over half a century now; on everything from the *tabula rasa* of childhood to the flow of world history.

These reflections take their cue from the universally entrenched paradigm of the African approach to matters of the cosmos, an approach encapsulated in wise sayings. But they replicate this mode only to a limited degree, preferring to stay off the more or less mysterious path - even if a number of reflections might end up projecting that *SAP* (Socratic-Aristotelian-Platonic) aura. As a collection, these reflections are not presented as philosophy, nay theology, pronounced from some celestial tower, but as simple prompts on the complexity and contradiction that is this phenomenon called life. They are no more than a demonstration of the often comic outcome when perfectly sensible philosophical anchors of life run against one another. When that occurs, the only logical counsel is to rise, dust off, grab on to yet another saying and move on; for that rain that beats the hell out of us must fall for our farms to flourish! Any such contradiction, then, need not be perceived as a negative in our approach to the project of living. If anything, it is meant to project *balance*, mentally and beyond, as the only meaningful *modus vivendi*.

Art is Man is art.

I am a man, perfect, not mad.

Every success hides many a failure.

There is no right or wrong, only time.

Right and wrong belong to the past but are shaped by the future.

It was indeed a true lie.

No do, no mistake*

Too much laughter can lead to tears.

Ah, power: I always wanted it, until I had it.

No one has nothing.

Wata noh get kontri*

Not all the dead are gone.

If you do not find pleasure in doing it, do not do it.

Sometimes, it is easier done than said.

The fly does not ask for an invitation to the chief's palace or party.

The skilled hunter does not carry on a chat whilst in the jungle.

A goat trying to pass for a gorilla is not only silly and salacious but sounds like the stuff much of life is made of.

I can handle it, I am African!

The mind is a minefield with multiple battles going on simultaneously.

Christmas, what a perfect season for *crises* and *mess*!

Die na njangi*

Woman wey yih sell njanga dear fit still fall stock*

*Living room.* So, all the other rooms in the house are not worth living in or what?

Do we open the window to let in fresh air or to let out foul air; do we build the fence to keep in or to keep out?

It is always right to err on the side of good.

Religion, how you continue to take the flack for the nation and every other thing – as if only you wear ravaging horns! If only they would look deep inside each of your houses to see the rainbow assembled around your dinner mat.

2

I appreciate your religion but my faith has taken up all the available space I had.

6 to 6 is not the same thing as 66.

The reveler and the pick-pocket have different motives for coming out to the party.

Some would be speechless but for their grandfathers.

To assert that some have no reading culture, now, it's not in our culture to be hard on others, is it? You mean all those shopping flyers they read count for nothing?

If you have to go to the farm for every spice then whose compound are you living in?

I never could get anything for my sister until the day I bought her that expensive one-of-a-kind designer beauty of a dress – to dress her corpse.

I got five additional dresses this year already. I will run out of closet space in no time if those deaths in the family continue at this rhythm.

My in-law went out with a bang, won't you agree? A designer suit worth more than all his clothes put together, and a brass band to accompany him to his last abode in a coffin more expensive than what passed for his home!

Instead of blaming those who profit from the dead how about advising those who would rather die than live?

My friends are always reproaching me for always receiving and never giving. They could not be more wrong, for the Spirits bear witness with me that I give a lot - of advice - and never do I bother to seek or receive any in return.

If only we knew who actually gave whom aid the world would be a different place.

You know you have become modern the moment you have a specialist to watch over every aspect of your life, including how to shit.

What difference does it make whether I am happy to see you sad or sad to see you happy?

As we move forward we must keep an eye on the past – if only to ensure it does not sneak up some of its sordid and inconvenient details on us.

You can conduct a discussion in the market but a market cannot conduct a discussion.

Did no one ever advise you never to stop someone who is suffering from diarrhea for a chat?

Citizens with some responsibilities – what an audacious (and stupid) suggestion?

The team that keeps possession of the ball longer stands a better chance of winning the football game.

Many rights are not innate but are born out of weakness.

I told her to prepare 5 kgs of bread for my breakfast. She went ahead and did. Gee, some folks can't take a joke seriously!

There is only one true science in man's existence: that of balance.

It is funny when a four year-old plays a forty year-old but it is silly when a forty year-old plays a four year-old. I wonder why?

*There is more joy in giving than in receiving*; that depends, are we talking about sex?

They keep asking me where I come from. I never answer because I never know, nor do they, which of the short or long answer they want.

You want to know why I sometimes feel like a prisoner with the rare favour to make love to his woman inside his cell knowing all too well the all-seeing guard is just on the other side of the door?

*Our differences make us stronger*, really? So, where did I come from with the impression that they make us weaker? Ah, it is that glass being half-empty or half-full thing, right?

It turned out I was absolutely right she was wrong.

Show an open bag and fowls will enter, freely, as long as they see grains of corn inside.

Some people talk as if they alone know where the cat mates. What can a man do about that?

I ran into my brother, a friend and this woman I had the hearts for - all in one day. When they each turned out to be fake, it hit me: every one must have at least a double somewhere on this planet,

Organic? I will shop and eat organic when I know what it means – or when I find one.

I never ran into a *politrician* who lost, only those whose lieing luck ran out.

Stories, no matter what we call them, are the foundation blocks upon which civilizations are built.

Many celebrities mistake their fame for possessing some higher ethical and moral standards. After all, who else is always stepping aside to *spend more time with* their *families*?

Life is a bit like my days: I can't say why, but I always seem to leave late when I get up early and early when I get up late.

She is always whining the fact that every time she buys something she finds it cheaper elsewhere. Well, come off it, my dear; that, in a nutshell, is life.

I love my freedom, and like that river, I will continue to travel alone - even as I meander.

They so believe in the individual they even signed over their national song to the individual.

I don't know about those who tell us not to fret over the small stuff. My big comes out of the small. So, how do they expect us to master the big stuff when it eventually blows up in our face because we ~~did not~~ neglected to take care of the small stuff?

Everybody is a product of everyone, and of everything else.

What comes free often goes undervalued.

Freedom is determined not so much by the ability to do or not do as by the ability to bear the consequence of what we do or do not do.

True freedom comes from the inside, not outside; is not defined but lived.

*Aim high and shoot low*, what cunning if not downright dishonest advice! How about aiming for where you intend to shoot?

*A bird in hand is worth two in the bush.* But you still have to go to the bush to catch that *one*.

Better at the end than at the beginning; that way, you stand a better chance of determining the outcome of the end you desire.

*Forgive and forget.* Before you buy that, be certain which of the hare or the tortoise you are in the tale of 'Let's kill our mothers.'

Sometimes the best help to give someone is no help at all.

The new generation in its wisdom will always sweep aside the old generation and its wisdom.

*Wisdom,* it is said, *comes with age.* We like it when we are called wise, but hate it when we are called old. Any wonder why foolishness continues to be our portion?

*Age is just a number:* another deception society has concocted to make us feel good about ourselves.

*Happy birthday?* Whom are we kidding? At the back of our minds is always that reminder that as our numbers are going up so too is our health going down. How can anyone be happy about that?

That is a lie. And believe me, that is the truth!

If we had to take the *esere* bean to speak we would all be dumb.

Get a grip on life before it gets a grip on you.

Only two generations are responsible for anything, the one before and the one after.

When it comes to building character, environment triumphs over man.

Virtue too stretched turns into vice.

*The big picture*? If I did not know a thing about it don't you think by now I would have changed my doctor because of his handwriting?

Advice is like medicine; it can make you better, or worse.

The world is huge, my brother; in some places, they cuddle, protect and raise baby boys to slaughter the pigs when these grow up.

How selfish can some get? To the extent of naming breeze and diseases after themselves, that how!

I got unassailable proof that this life is, indeed, full of mysteries - as when a Republican Party of today is the Democratic Party of yesterday.

Never debate, negotiate or play with a man who shares the same name with his animal or whose name changes from West to North and back every time: that would be like trying to catch fish with your bare hands.

She said I should ask for Piggie upon arrival: when she left, it was clear in my mind whether I was going or not.

'I am just down here in my home,' said the grass. 'Well, what the heck,' said the two elephants.

That life is a jungle, you know, but do you know what to do?

Tell me, which animal is the lion's friend? Yes, what a life!

Do you love the lion for its bravery and power? Do you detest it for making a prey out of the colourful, beautiful zebra?

Soap did you say? To wash a pot in which fufu was prepared? Really?

We are members of a team; still, we must play different positions for the team to win.

Even a consensus is never a willing horse.

No matter what, fingers never miss the way to the mouth.

We must keep hope alive; it keeps us alive.

When you are looking for an address you slow down your speed, or do you not?

The steadiest place to stand, always, is the middle.

On the virtue of balance, well, you are looking at one who crosses the hanging bridge everyday.

Love, words and children are like water, any one of them can kill you, or make you well.

At fifteen we dream, at fifty, we live, and at ninety we relive.

At fifteen, we have our life ahead of us; at fifty, ahead and behind us, and at ninety, behind us.

Tomorrow will always be better than today.

*Better late than never*? It all depends what kind of late we are talking about.

Jesse ran so that Barack could win.

Things change when people do.
Thought is to action what a foundation is to a well-built house.

When building a foundation, which do you put first: stones, sand or cement?

Every virtue has a vice with which it conjugates.

The venom of the mamba is the treatment for its bite.

Even our satans we must bury.

Small minds fear a big idea; it can swallow them.

Because it is called a right does not necessarily make it right.

I would rather recover the loot than catch the thief.

No one is good at everything, I said, trying to soothe my son for not making the school band. No one is good at everything, he said in his defence, when he returned home weeks after with a string of Fs on his report card.

Do not take on life like the hare, else do not be surprised if you find yourself behind the tortoise – like the hare.

*My mind is playing tricks on me*, I hear every now and again. If it truly is your mind, I say get a grip on it!
A true friend pillories and pampers where others would rather only one.

I said I was your friend, not necessarily a true one, did I? Are you surprised I did not tell you that your breath stinks and that you snore?

Rock can become dust as dust can become rock – with circumstance.

Be careful when you spit into the atmosphere; the spittle could fall back unto your face.

A dance, even crooked, says more than a thousand words.

How much can the mind rely on the mouth?

To sleep with one eye open is not the same thing as to stay awake with one eye shut.

They almost failed to take the lawyer for a liar when they realized what a fool is who expects the chameleon to suddenly become a snake!

Sure, I can give you more than one reason why every disappointment is a blessing. Just give me a moment to think!

I seek to understand these *humbled*, *surprised* and *not worthy* folks when they are bestowed with some award. They alone are from Planet Earth while the rest of us must be some extra-terrestrials.

I don't have any answer for this but I always know it when I get an answer right.

Until that day when the student begins to evaluate the teacher there shall continue to be, no mincing, malice, pestilence and war.

Who defines, determines, distributes and, when he pleases, destroys.

Yes, the man drenched in the rain can urinate with his pants up.

Laughter and tears may not dwell in the same house but do the same compound.

Go ahead, take an issue with *order*. That man was not born to be a robot in any way? And you would be right!

Clothes some put on to look desirable, others to appear undesirable.

Some dress to impress; others, just to cover the mess.

I question that wisdom that says I should listen to a man tell me about the road to a village he has never traveled.

The moon and the sun both give brightness to what is underneath them, but they are not the same.

Sometimes the eyes insist on staying open when you would want them shut and shut when you would rather they stay open.

Gentlemen, the next time someone asks how you are doing, point to the top of your head

My wife takes seven hours to do her hair anytime we are to go out. Go ahead and charge me with anything but lack of patience.

*Friends*, some say, *are better than money;* yeah, until these friends eat your money!

I hear your counsel never to let anything, especially money, come between me and my friends; While we are at it, I pledge never to allow anything come between me and the green one.

Would I ever consider pushing out my relatives if that meant reigning in on my blood pressure, you ask? Hmh, the proposition sounds too good to be true.

*If you want to prosper and be happy, pay no attention nor listen to others.* Once I have that established, I will find out if that includes teachers, parents or even Nature and deities.

What a way with words we humans have! *Starting a family.* Right! Your family got wiped out by a plague, or you fell from the sky!

Latin: to feel learned, to sound stupid.

One indispensable tool for the lady: the mirror - for good or bad?

It never dawned on me how too much goodwill could kill until the last time when I fell ill; all my friends became my doctor, all of a sudden. 'E.f, have you tried honey mixed with raw egg yolk?' said one. 'How about a mixture of lemon, whisky and organic banana warmed for 2 minutes?' said another. Thank the Spirits, I did not even have the energy to go put together any of the suicidal concoctions!

Thank God for those big intertribal wars in Europe they call world wars; we are left struggling with only five thieves and impostors in my father's compound.

Grains of sand stuck together can surpass the force of a rock.

You must be a diviner, right? How else do you expect to put out fire with more fire?

Have you ever noticed something about those who are always saying money is not everything?

As I searched all over for my pen, she asked me where I had it last. I looked up and thought, 'E.f, time to work on those magical qualities some folks obviously think you possess.'

Even the man who is down has an obligation not to pick and hand a stick to the one who is standing over and flogging the hell out of him.

When you *turn the other cheek* be careful not to twist the neck.

Listen to your doctor, your teacher and your boss. Listen to your parents and pastor; even listen to your banker. Above all, listen to your Spirit.

The material may change our life circumstance, the intellect our outlook toward that circumstance.

Harmony is having what you want to have and becoming what you want to become.

Downpression is a Sword of Damocles – if and when the downpressed know it.

When did our fear transform into respect?

To the greatest purveyor of terror in the world we, the people, flock daily to enter. Something must be wrong with the country - or with us!

With all its extraordinary qualities, the lion can never bring up the deer.

Do not enter the bush and you won't be pierced by thorns.

Good and Bad owe their existence to each other.

Friendship is blessed; it got only two things ready to screw it out of shape: money and the opposite sex.

Look at that tree, broad and tall; it thinks it constitutes a forest as a result.

The day we began to care more what public officials do in private and less what private individuals do in public is the day the rain began to beat upon us.

How I love to get to work early and stay late. My boss is always sending accolades my way as a result. If only he knew the fact that the office is but the lesser of my two hells.

You don't insult a woman by telling her that she squats to urinate.

Workaholics are playing with fire; they are certainly not playing God. For God's sake, even God rested.

Get rest! Even God did!

Life, cyclical ever this wheel – like dust that turns to rock and back to dust again.

I now have incontrovertible evidence life can be unfair. How can one guy have a whole sentence for a name - all by himself? Henri Martial Rakotoarimanana Rajaonalinarimpiana!

So, what's the big deal that I forget a few things every now and then? I do remember many others in their place, don't I?

I am living proof of the fact that life abhors a vacuum. Every time I forget something, I remember something else in its place.

This is a fact, stated with no pride. I never forget anything; I simply remember something else.

*Going back and forth*? Not me. I would rather wait to get forth to whatever it is before thinking of getting back

It makes no freaking difference whether you call shit stool.

Stressed up trying to get used to that new technology? Not me. I simply sit back and before you know it, it is history, cast aside by yet another new technology.

To all those out there who believe, for whatever reason, that they are stronger, busier, smarter, nobler, better or whatever than the other, I say to try walking in the other's shoe for even a day.

You are free to shout during a discussion, but that would be like spitting into an ocean.

The fox says it is clever; if only it knew who were teaching its offspring!

Drop a fish in clean or dirty water and it will try to swim.

The only victory against the force of hormones is death.

The awe is not that man has reached the moon; it is in how he has, casually, flown over billions in squatters to get there.

If we knew when we were going to lose something would we lose it?

So the fingers of both hands meet at the back from only one angle; for that, you want to drag your Maker before your guru?

*Let your conscience be your guide*? And then what happens to our mass media and our vice gods from the west, north and elsewhere?

*Life is too short to be filled with sorrow.* Really?
Short or long, is it and can it be life without sorrow?

*Here today, gone tomorrow*, I often hear it uttered like some regret at what is to come. I say where is our sense of adventure? Or are we now chickening out of our change- is-good mantra?

*The best things in life*, they say, *are free*; unfortunately, many cannot pay the price of that freedom.

I have this problem with freedom; I don't know what it feels or looks like.

True freedom never comes free.

Life is a patchwork of multiple quilts: biology, chemistry, economics, relations, circumstance....

Life is like the market to which we go with a calabash of palm oil and return with a bundle of shrimps.

Life is a trinity of the unborn, the dead and the living.

Life is a lottery – gamble on!

There are no anti-gamblers in life; it is a lottery everyone must play.

Life is one kind of a lottery where your wins and losses have nothing to do with how many tickets you bought, or did not buy.

Life is like being in an airplane caught in a de-pressurizing situation; you are strongly counseled to put on your own mask before attempting to put anyone else's.

Be careful with Life – it can kill you before you have time to live!

Ah, life! Where are we looking, into the mirror or through the glass?

Life, where did we keep our eyes? Can we see you whole, ever?

Life is like changing clothes; whatever it is, you can't and shouldn't put on the same thing every day.

In a way, life is like driving; however zig-zag it may be going, only mine do I trust.

Marriage, that murderer love struggles to survive with.

They say marriage is give-and-take; now, who gives and who takes – that is the question.

Marriage, one must admit, has this one nice thing to its credit; you know, instantly, who is responsible when something goes wrong.

If anyone has a reason why these two should not be united in (holy) matrimony, *speak now or forever hold your tongue*. I think I get the second but I am still to figure out the first part.

If anyone has a reason why these two should not be united in (holy) matrimony, *speak now or forever hold your tongue*. I get the second part. As for the first, are you kidding me? I came here to have a good time, not to commit suicide.

If anyone has a reason why these two should not be united in (holy) matrimony, *speak now or forever hold your tongue*. I came here to watch these two each embark on the path to mutual suicide, not to join them.

Do I hear folks I would otherwise call normal, any day, swear,'I have never gambled – and never will – in my life?'And behold, they are married!

Who says it not great, marriage? But for it life we would go through thinking we had no faults at all. Nothing like marriage to bring us to our knees and make us realize how always wrong we are!

Marriage is to love as water is to oil.

Marriage or love? Stop being selfish, my friends, and choose.

Marriage, love's prisoner.

Now we know, at least half the things said about marriages are untrue.

Wow, I just celebrated 30 years of married bliss; ten each with Clementina, Evangelina and Mojoko.

Love, the pinnacle of our follies, where babies seek to play adults and adults are content to be babies.

Love is like Lagos, that huge dazzling African city, to which we continue to flock - and get entrapped.

Despite the overwhelming evidence surrounding us we still go ahead and *fall* in love; either we are the most stupid beings or the most hopeless optimists.

*Love is blind.* Little wonder it keeps falling victim to our caprices time and time again?

Ah love, where self-annointed angels seek non-existent angels.

Life and love are like eating; if you don't sit up well while you eat, the food can start a war in your stomach.

Life, love – it's not a science. Why spend so much time analyzing and not enough time to live and love?

As would be expected, not even graduates of the I-Me-My-Mine school have succeeded to turn marriage on its head and make it anything but the community bond that it is.

Searching for, finding, making, falling in, falling out… Ah, love, and the things we do in your name!

The world is huge. In some places they define as custody battle when a wife fights her husband over the cheque, sorry, child; well, through the cheque.

So-called love and marriage in the millennium: one percent human and ninety-nine percent legal.

When it comes to the affairs between a man and woman it is not dishonest to advice that the right thing to do, as a friend, is not to say the right thing – unless you intend to commit suicide or become a matyr!

My friend just celebrated another milestone, and from every indication, the *Just Divorced* card I sent her, again, was well received.

To all those seeking to recover from love's cruel punches, what better to recommend than a Lovers Annonymous Incorporated membership?

Because the new will always replace the old, a constant in life is the struggle to be on the side of the new; that's the only way to ensure relevance – and life.

(Self) education is the nail on freedom's finger.

*Speak the truth and shame the devil.* And incur the wrath of our angels!

Dine with anyone garbed in "rights" with a long spoon.

Tradition stacked up against Modernity? It's more like Tradition versus God incarnate.

Human rights, yes; how about some human values?

God made man; then man made his god, in Europe, and sent him to New York, New England, New Zealand, New Glasgow, New France…

England? Britain? Great Britain? United Kingdom…Queendom? I am as confused as you – and they!

*Curiosity killed the cat.* Or so it thought. It forgot *the cat has nine lives.*

The heart, the head and the hands – when they agree – are formidable allies.

You don't eat okro soup everyday of your life, do you? So, how come you only dine with that man garbed in 'rights'?

Ah, humans and our way with words! When we say a 99 year old's accidental death is a "tragic loss" what exactly are we saying?

Where do you prefer your cargo, hung on your chest or strung between your legs?

This cargo is a must and you can have it emaciated or lifeless – what shall it be?

The pig was given a golden ring, and what did it do with it?

The iguana does not go swimming in hot water just because it has a protective skin.

At 15 she will die for the sweetheart; at 25 she will work the horse; at 35 she just wants to kill the pig; at 45

– if the pig survives – she simply replaces with a new pet. And at 55…..

*Change is good* is the mantra from cradle to grave. If change is that good, why don't we ever stick to any change we adopt?

*Unlike poles attract, like poles repel.* How about birds of the same feather; do they flock together?

For a good life, a good heart and head are destined as life partners.

No longer do I know how nor what to speak

What business have balls on the chest with balls between the legs?

When the *ngila\** reaches crescendo even the awkward shoulders are not shy to quiver.

*Your life in your hands* – you're sure it's a safe bet? How about in your head, or better still, solidly sealed inside your heart?

That *life begins at fifty*? Well, now I can begin to unmake all the mistakes I've made thus far.

My life continues to be a wreck and whereas only angels cross my path on a daily basis. I swear, something must be wrong somewhere, somehow, and I struggle to find out with whom.

The devils of the *good old days* would easily pass for saints today.

Life does not change; people do.

What does it say about life that the one standing in the light, often, cannot see the one standing in the dark?

The whole city now seems to own a Sahara brand - after I got one. Am I a trend-setter or what!

Don't you just love this game, Love? With its one and simple rule – no rules! That way, you never know when you win or lose. And do you care?

Love and country have a few things in common: permanent interests, their liberating and suffocating capacity.

I tried to cross the road in heavy traffic to meet my friend who tried to cross from the other side to meet me. The absence of (self) control – to it we charge most early graves.

Love, *the more you give, the more you receive*, they say. Well, just make sure you don't sit up too late waiting to receive love back from where you sent it as it has a way of sneaking up on you from places and when you least expect!

Love, like beauty, *is in the eyes of the beholder*; sometimes, even our best loving effort will be received like shit!

Kindness is not *njangi**

*Don't be childish*, grow up, we often hear the reproach. I say more power to childishness if it that means staving the hate and other matured harvests, so called, of adulthood.

Cursing me I did not reciprocate your act of kindness? Please, just be content that I kept the circle going by extending kindness to someone else.

Fifty is the new forty, really? So, why am I feeling ninety-nine and afraid of sitting anywhere near a young woman?

What can be so good about falling, even if it is in love?

I hate love so much I am a five-time divorcee.

'Love me for who I am, not for who you think I should be.' And after that I will ensure that you become what I want you to become!

Love, you continue to send arrows and spears through our hearts, and we continue to sing odes to you; who is the fool?

If you want to continue to love a woman, do not marry her.

This fiction called love is real, indeed.

'Love me based on the inside, not by how I look on the outside.' I say bullshit to such stupidity that will make a man seek to fall inside that thing without knowing or paying attention to what it looks like on the outside.

'Love me based on the inside, not by how I look on the outside.' I say amen to that: let's go inside so that I can bear witness to what the inside is like!

Who says the child's world is easy? Imagine that two-year-old trying to figure whether *tonton* is a *he* or *she*.

*There is light at the end of the tunnel.* I say I don't care for any light that would rather hide in a tunnel.

What if not the height of selfishness, to demand love! We should give, and receive with opens arms, if it comes (back) our way.

I have always preferred the top to the bottom – of anything good. So, instead of *from the bottom*, how about thanking me from the *top of your heart*?

Along the narrow forest path, where should a man walk, in front or behind his child?

Newspapers, they might be papers but they are far from news.

Because we should not go through life as if death did not matter does not mean we should go through life as if death is all there is to it.

Mostly left to rot, I am resurrected - at funerals. Poetry, I am.

Forty and feeling forlorn? Write poetry.

The challenge in communication is to determine whether what is said is more significant than what is not said.

Does anyone doubt that America is a free country? Who else is this free to do as she pleases across the globe?

'Sorry for your loss,' he said. 'I just finished guzzling down a crate of beer all by myself. Good to go, I'd say – till another funeral rolls around.'

The one who is always speaking first, fastest and loudest is the one with something and the most to hide; often.

It is the onset of madness when a man begins to answer every question he is posing.

Everyone is concerned about me and I still cannot feel fine.

Some folks always complain there is not enough love in the world. Then, they turn around and blame me for spreading it around. I wish they would just make up their bloody minds.

Running around and shouting 'I'm free' – even in bachannal style – does not necessarily make it so.

How unwise is it to go searching for your woman with a blowing horn!

What is the difference between people in free countries and those in unfree countries? Those in free countries believe the lies their governments feed them with; those in unfree countries do not.

What is the safest place to stand to insult the lion, you ask? Keep thinking.

*Marriage*, the widow now charged in the murder of her *love*.

The *good ol' days*? They are old but certainly were nothing to write home about.

*Age is just a number*, yes, and a bad one at that.

Short cuts in life? Sure, if you are ready for the bumps and potholes.

Do your brain a favour; do not force to remember that which is not important. If it is important, you will remember!
*You are the sunshine of my life*; just don't burn me.

Can't say if sweeter than the one inside my throat, but *you are the apple of my eye,* all the same.

Fleeing to the moon; what a fantastic flight from reality.

*The truth shall set you free*; even if it causes you pain.

Africa finally began to get into me the moment I was forced to get out of Africa.

*I am a good listener.* I say, good for you. I am a good talker. After all, someone has to step up in place of all these dumb pretending to pass for sages, right?

If truly *life begins at fifty,* I say what a relief! For those under fifty, hurry not; for those over fifty, time to begin to unmake all the mistakes we've made thus far.

The *silent majority.* And how on earth did anyone know it's the majority?

The heart is the door into my house; let's not forget my eyes, mouth!

The more you give the more you shall receive. All I seek to know is where this all begins – the receiving or the giving end.

*I tip my hat off to you.* And you think you have done it? How about prostrating on the floor so I can walk all over you?

Whatever happened to child discipline, you ask?   We *timed* (it) *out*; after all, we don't know any better than children, do we?

*Spare the rod and spoil the child*; in some places, they take *tough love* to mean *time out!*

Demanding and expecting principles in life? Now, how judgemental is that!

The problem with politics is to know when principles, the people or the politicians are the problem.

Because you can do it does not mean you should do it.

Good deeds pay, and so do bad deeds.

The veil may hide what we don't want others to see; it may also hide what we don't want to see.

How can we tell whether that ten year old's strength is for real when he keeps picking only on five year olds in the playground?

*That's all Greek to me!* No, it's not; not if you understand the English language.

How unfair is it to the Greeks with everyone scurrying to speak the English language and no one Greek!
Most days I feel like Greek, the foundation of the house, but the house all the same that has been totally abandoned by my owners.

Ignorance is strength, and so is knowledge.

What is a flower if not an adorned weed or plant with a name?

Our preference for the truth over a lie has been greatly exaggerated.

Life, definitely, is not all it is cranked up to be. What it is, I would tell you – if I knew.

Life is a school that never graduates its students.

I will do nothing but right the day I graduate from the school of life; for now, bear with me.

Whether it's habit, tradition, custom or values, it's all the same. We need only substitute the individual, organization, social group or country with one or the other.

*Making the best of a bad situation*: what more perfect example in real life than in marriage, sorry, the institution of marriage.

Freedom, we gain one, we lose one; so, let's keep at the task, folks.

You have hardly known how to navigate through life until you have, repeatedly eaten – or tried to share a meal - out of the same bowl with your brothers.

*Where did (the) time go?* Absolutely nowhere!

Enemies are good if not for the fact that, but for them, we would have no one to blame for our mistakes and transgressions.

He is loud, but he is saying nothing.

Tell me if you necessarily see better because there is a dazzling sunshine out there?

Brainwashing, education or propaganda - it's one and the same thing. What it is called depends on who is doing the calling.

That something down there can take one high up there, well, that must be one of the mysteries of this life – like the poor sustaining the rich.

It is good counsel to insist that only those who have erred need give counsel.

Yes to the past and to the present. But the future – how can we tell if there is really such a thing?

The working class and the ruling class. Before you swallow that, consider the amount of work it takes the ruling class to keep the working class working.

Friendship happens; don't interfere, and don't sweat it.

Who teaches sex? Who learns sex, really?

My car depreciates while his house appreciates everyday; how fair is that?

Begging has never been this hard. Maybe it's time all the beggars consider moving to the doorsteps of churches, mosques, synagogues and temples.

Friendship is more important than money. One of the few things I am certain about is who it is that is making such a statement.

*Time and tide wait for no one.* Good, because I would not wish to be in the company of a tide, any day.

A man's home is his castle – until it becomes his prison.

*Beauty is in the inside.* Too bad, because I can't see it.

*Opportunity comes but once*; says who?

What strengthens us can also weaken us.

The tussle is to ensure love's selfish side does not get the better of us.

Because we are near to the object does not necessarily mean we shall see it clearer.

Nothing like convention to put the brakes on living!

Everything looks beautiful from afar.

Elections – a perfect opportunity for us to ensure our freedom to complain about those we vote for.

*Behind every successful man is a woman.* And behind every unsuccessful man, there is…?

Consider every advice before you accept or reject it, including this one.

Advice does not have to pleasant; it should be honest.

Death might be the ultimate and perfect solution to all my woes but, I bet you, it is one solution I fight hard every day to avoid implementing.

You cannot know good if you have not known bad.

Love, the game we all liable to play at some point in life.

Nothing gets me more scared to eat than hearing *'you are what you eat.'*

So, you want us to pat you on the back for taking the horse to the stream even if you could not get it to drink?

Time offers no guarantee as to the cure of the wound. It offers nothing but hope, which can easily turn sour leading to the festering of the wound.

Because man is mercurial, consider social justice as a road, not a destination.

Some are asleep even in the day; others are awake even at night.

Without a gong, yours is but a whisper in the market square.

Spread the love in words and deeds; you were not meant to be alone. Not even God wished to be alone. If he did, he would not have created the world.

There must be only two kinds of people in my universe; those wicked ones who always call me old and those friendly fellows who tell me how good I (still) look in my sixties.

*Time waits for no one. The patient dog eats the fattest bone.* Now, go reconcile those two!

Religion segregates, and congregates.

No one and nothing is everything.

Everything that love is, it is not.

*Love conquers all* – even sanity, royals and common sense.
I am man, perfect, and no labels.

It is not by repeatedly saying a stream is an ocean that it will turn into one.

To impregnate you must penetrate and ejaculate.

Love can heal the wound created by love.

Like a machine, the body must be tuned off every now and then to retain the efficacy of its parts.

*He who is down fears no fall.* But he should fear being trampled upon should he be feeble in getting back on his feet.

Love is a two-sided weapon.

Democracy, that wonderfully-package gift that allows us to make noise to get ignored – and to feel on top of the world about it. Yes, it's *democrazy*!

*Actions speak louder than words*; and inaction too.

Talk may be cheap, but not when your life depends on it.

The falling tree trunk does not ask the branches if they feel like going down with it.

Nothing like love to make us small – and young. And who would take issue with that?

Fear - the worst form of respect, and it can never be relied upon.

To think I forgive every harm you do to me out of the kindness of my heart, well, that's your business. My business is the survival of my heart and, quite frankly, my being.

The world is screwed, and for this we have our angels to thank.

For what it's worth, children are the only natural humans I know; no make-up whatsoever – until adults come into the picture, to fix things.

I will complain all I want about this life; after all, I did not ask to be born.

Birthdays – happy are they who have to worry over the farce only once every four years.

Our saints owe their status to us, satans.

*If wishes were horses, beggars would ride* – if beggars could afford.

Ah love, you got what it takes to take what I got.

*Money can't buy love.* And it shouldn't; after all, what is there that is so special worth buying?

It is good to treat the sickness; it is better to treat the cause
Honesty is the best policy; save it!

How true is it that truth is our most important value?

Puff-puff tink say na yih one sweet with ngapsa.*

I know a great deal about Tolerance; it got me into this mess.

I do not give a damn if life is a stage with us as actors;
In the next play, I want to be the director, why not the script writer?

Life can never be a referendum.

Wisdom comes with age and ages with it.

Oil can bear a grudge against soap only for so long, knowing fully well that it is at the base of soap's existence.

*There are plenty of fishes in the sea*; that includes sharks.

*Are you alright?* she asked after I fell and bloodied a knee against an iron pole. I said to myself, 'Sure, I am alright; after all, I did not die, if that is what you mean.'

Life is like hunger and hope is the food that takes care of it.

Your financial advisor wants to make you rich: well, have you found out how rich he is?

Ah love, this wonderful thing that kills!

Maybe not the apple of the eye, but men and women are the centre of the others's universe – their conversations, jokes, sorrows, even poetry. And you dare to imagine one can live without the other?

Since the garden of Eden, the universes and fortunes of man and woman are stuck together – for better or for worse.

That woman came after man in the garden of Eden? Well, she very quickly gained ground and in no time began to lead man, by the …well, to this day.

*You may now kiss the bride.* Where have you been, pastor? I have been kissing her severally – and even more – to this moment.

The public and the private now inhabit the same space.

Truth, how haughty you have become! That only you stand on the pedestal of Right! How would you like to know that our preference for you over that lie has not only been greatly exaggerated but that you alone cannot make the forest, no matter your enormity.

I am a saint – or close to one. I know it, because I am poor, powerless – and politically correct.

Is it a bird because it flies or because it has wings and feathers?

I exploded out of my Atlantic Guinea, Equatorial Guinea and Sahara Guinea suit a long time ago; it became too tiny, too tight and, quite frankly, too suffocating.

Ah, how our differences have kept us in peace!

English or French, it's your choice; poli*trician* or politi-*chien, it leaves a sour taste no matter the language it is eaten in*?

Say everything you think and you will be called anything but good.

Even our satans have merit.

I am more than a man.

A progressive: one who cannot make up his mind; is everywhere and nowhere; swims with ease, walks with difficulty; is a banana leaf in the wind. And this is not saying much!

Everyone is with and for the people, until we get on top, and then, the people become excess baggage.

Many are those who will vouch for the truth; fewer are those who will die for it.

I am often chided for always focusing on the negatives. In my defence, I ask, how else do I turn the negatives into positives if not by focusing all my attention on them?

One regret, one blame, one hope after another; that's the art of living for you.

What do regret, blame and hope have in common? They form the trilogy of each and every of our responses in this project called living.

Looking at the map of Africa I am struck by the absence of space to write in the names of all those countries. So many there that one is forced to, simply, throw or drop some of these names out there in the surrounding oceans!

Kudos to all these our angels who are always *giving back to society*; they've succeeded in making the rest of us look like disciples of satan.

We humans can be weird: imagine always insisting on knowing whether that newborn is male or female, when all we are going to say in reply is 'wonderful'.

*It is my business and my business alone*: one of the biggest myths any society can wrap around itself.

The power game is to always rush to make things not right but a right; that way you are certain to always place yourself on the pinnacle of the human jungle food chain. So, every time your hands are tied, turn around and scream, 'You're free!' It can never hurt.

I need someone to lean on, feed on and from, copy from…. No, I did not say I am a parasite!

What is the use of even sugar with no tea to drink with?

'*Why can't you ever make up your mind?*' Because I am flexible, adaptable to change, go with the flow; need I go on?

*It is entirely in your hands.* Well, my hands can't do nothing about anything. How about entrusting it to my brains?

The way you talk about your mutual friend to your fiend is the way your friend will talk to your mutual friend about you.

For every success there is a multitude of failures.

The child you lock up in the room for stealing cannot go to fetch you water from the village stream.

It is more than dreams; it is your anchor to life.

Because you live in a forest, you think that qualifies you as a hunter?

Looking at today's civilized world, one is struck by the rising rates of insemination, C-section births, and female celibacy that is catching up with that of Roman Catholic priests. With all these, one cannot help but wonder, has the importance of the vagina been greatly exaggerated?

The real deal? To seek to love, not as a quid pro quo, but as a bargain.

Words are swords, and ploughshares.

*Private parts*, did you say? And what about the others? Do they belong to someone else?

# Glossary

*Die na njangi* [lit. We each have our turn to die]: *Njangi* is a custom across parts of the African World whereby a group of individuals (with some shared central identity) come together, usually on a monthly basis, contribute funds and hand over to one member at a time. The intent of the funds is to help members invest. Referred to also as *esusu, isusu, pari,* etc.

*esere* – among the Kalabari (of Nigeria) and neighbouring ethnic groups, poisonous bean administered to a person suspected of a serious breach of social peace (e.g, witchcraft). The person's innocence is assumed (upheld) if s/he does not drop dead following the (public) eating of the bean.

*ngila* – among the Nkongho-Mbos of Cameroon, a dance form in which young men demonstrate their acrobatic dancing skills; for the admiration of maidens!

*No do, no mistake*: There is room for mistake only as long as one tries (to do something). Of course, not doing anything (out of a fear of making a mistake) is a sure recipe for inertia.

*politrician* – pejorative coinage (from *politics* and *tricks*).

*Wata noh get kontri:* No one can truly lay claim to a body of water. To transpose, the parallel can be drawn to the individual whose action is totally independent of the influence of others.

*Woman wey yih sell njanga dear fit still fall stock:* Going for quick and too much profit [in one shot] is no guarantee for a thriving business in the long run. Not to be taken literally.

*Puff-puff tink say na yih one sweet with ngapsa.* No matter how highly we think of ourselves, none amongst us possesses a monopoly of any virtue whatsoever.